A Conversation wit

A Conversation with Harris and Seldon

RALPH HARRIS
ARTHUR SELDON
with Stephen Erickson

WITH COMMENTARIES BY
ALASTAIR BURNET
MILTON FRIEDMAN
HERBERT GIERSCH
PETER HENNESSY
ANTONY JAY
ANTONIO MARTINO
PASCAL SALIN
GORDON TULLOCK

iea

The Institute of Economic Affairs

First published in Great Britain in 2001 by
The Institute of Economic Affairs
2 Lord North Street
Westminster
London SW1P 3LB
in association with Profile Books Ltd

Copyright © The Institute of Economic Affairs 2001

The moral right of the authors has been asserted.

All rights reserved. Without limiting the rights under copyright reserved above, no part of this publication may be reproduced, stored or introduced into a retrieval system, or transmitted, in any form or by any means (electronic, mechanical, photocopying, recording or otherwise), without the prior written permission of both the copyright owner and the publisher of this book.

A CIP catalogue record for this book is available from the British Library.

ISBN 0 255 36498 9

Many IEA publications are translated into languages other than English or are reprinted. Permission to translate or to reprint should be sought from the General Director at the address above.

Typeset in Stone by MacGuru
info@macguru.org.uk

Printed and bound in Great Britain by Hobbs the Printers

CONTENTS

The authors	7
Editor's introduction	11
Foreword by John Blundell	13
The theme of the conversation, by Stephen Erickson	19

The Conversation   25

Commentaries   67

1. Spies in the night?   67
   Sir Alastair Burnet
2. The IEA's influence in our times   70
   Milton Friedman
3. The IEA and its indirect influence abroad   73
   Herbert Giersch
4. A team of singular impact   76
   Peter Hennessy
5. *Yes, Minister* and the IEA   77
   Sir Antony Jay
6. Stupor mundi: the IEA and its impact   81
   Antonio Martino
7. The IEA and the advance to classical liberalism   85
   Pascal Salin

8 The intellectual situation in the United States   88
   in the post-war years and the influence
   of the IEA
   Gordon Tullock

About the IEA   92

THE AUTHORS

Sir Alastair Burnet

Alastair Burnet was Editor of *The Economist* (1965–74), Editor of *The Daily Express* (1974–6), and Associate Editor, Independent Television News (1982–91). He was previously a leader writer on *The Glasgow Herald* (1951–8), Commonwealth Fund Fellow in the USA (1956–7) and leader writer on *The Economist* (1958–63). He was knighted in 1984, and has won awards from the British Academy of Television Arts (in 1965, 1970 and 1979) and the Royal Television Society (in 1981 and 1999). He has been on the board of Times Newspapers Holdings Ltd since 1982, and is a former member of the Council of the Banking Ombudsman, the Monopolies and Mergers Commission and the board of United Racecourses Ltd.

Herbert Giersch

Herbert Giersch was awarded his doctorate at Münster University in 1948, and his habilitation at Münster followed in 1950. He became Professor of Economics at the Saar University in Saarbrücken, was President of Kiel Institute of World Economics from 1969 to 1989 and is now Professor Emeritus of Economics at the University of Kiel. He has received many awards (Ludwig Erhard Award, Paolo Baffi International Prize for Economics, Prognos

Award, Great Cross of Merit and Star and Sash of the Federal Republic of Gemany, Joachim Jungius Medal, August Loesch Ring of Honour), three honorary doctorates and several fellowships. He established the Herbert Giersch Foundation in 1998. His many publications include *The World Economy in Perspectives: Essays on International Trade and European Integration* (1999) and *Openness for Prosperity: Essays in World Economics* (1993).

Milton Friedman

Milton Friedman received the Nobel Memorial Prize for Economic Science in 1976, and the National Medal of Science and the Presidential Medal of Freedom in 1988. He served as an unofficial adviser to presidential candidate Barry Goldwater and Presidents Nixon and Reagan. He is currently a Senior Research Fellow at the Hoover Institute at Stanford University and a Professor Emeritus of Economics at the University of Chicago, where he taught from 1946 to 1976. The University of Chicago Press recently published his and his wife's memoirs, *Two Lucky People*.

Peter Hennessy

Peter Hennessy has been Professor of Contemporary History at Queen Mary and Westfield College, University of London since 1992. Before that he held various visiting and research posts at British and overseas universities. From 1972 to 1991 he was a journalist, working on *The Times*, the *Financial Times*, *The Economist*, the *New Statesman* and the *Independent*. He has written and presented numerous television and radio programmes and is the author of many books on British politics and the constitution. He has honorary degrees from the Universities of the West of England, Westminster and Kingston.

Sir Antony Jay

After reading classics at Cambridge, Antony Jay joined the BBC in 1955. He was editor of the daily topical *Tonight* programme before leaving to become a freelance writer. In 1972 he and John Cleese founded Video Arts, the comedy training film company which also produced Milton Friedman's *Free to Choose* series. He also wrote, with Jonathan Lynn, *Yes, Minister* and *Yes, Prime Minister*, the TV comedy series about collision and collusion in the corridors of power.

Antonio Martino

Antonio Martino is a Member of the Italian Parliament and Professor of Economics in the Department of Political Science, LUISS University, Rome. He was Italy's Minister of Foreign Affairs in 1994 and is a founding member of Forza Italia, Italy's largest party. He is a member of the Foreign Relations Committee in the Chamber of Deputies and President of the Italian Group of the Inter-Parliamentary Union. He is a member of the Mont Pèlerin Society and was its president from 1988 to 1990. He is the author of twelve books and over 150 articles on economic theory and policy. His latest books include *Economia e liberta* (1996) and *Stato padrone* (1997). His honours include Grand'Ufficiale, Ordine al Merito della Repubblica Italiana, 1993; Gran Croce, Special Class, Knights of Malta, 1995; and an honorary doctorate from F. Marroquin University, Guatemala, 1997.

Pascal Salin

Pascal Salin is Professor of Economics at the Université Paris-Dauphine. He was president of the Mont Pèlerin Society from 1994 to 1996. He has been an editor of several books and has contributed to many books, reviews and newspapers. He has been a consultant in various organisations, and his most recent books are *La vérité sur la monnaie* (Odile Jacob, 1990), *Macroéconomie* (PUF, 1991), *Libre-échange et protectionnisme* (PUF, 1991), *La concurrence* (PUF, 1995), *L'arbitraire fiscal* (Editions Michel Slatkine, 1996) and *Libéralisme* (Odile Jacob, 2000).

Gordon Tullock

Gordon Tullock received his JD in 1947 and an honorary Ph.D. in 1994, both from the University of Chicago. He is a Distinguished Fellow of the American Economic Association (1998), and has been a major contributor to the development of the theoretical underpinnings of public choice. Tullock's hypotheses, Tullock's laws and Tullock's paradoxes have shaped the development of public choice, as well as charting new areas in law and economics and sociobiology. Beginning with publications in the *Journal of Political Economy* and the *American Economic Review*, Tullock has published over 160 articles (not counting reprints and translations), 130 communications and 20 books.

EDITOR'S INTRODUCTION

In 1999, The Liberty Fund of Indianapolis, Indiana, produced in its 'Intellectual Portraits' series a video of a conversation in which Lord Harris of High Cross and Dr Arthur Seldon CBE answered questions from Professor Stephen Erickson about their work at the IEA, as General Director and Editorial Director respectively, from the founding of the Institute until the late 1980s.

The video contains many insights into the difficulties of founding and running an institute proclaiming free market ideals at a time when conventional wisdom was hostile to such ideas. It shows how Ralph Harris and Arthur Seldon overcame resistance from the establishment and gradually, by force of argument, turned opinion in favour of markets.

So that these insights can reach a wider audience, Occasional Paper 116 reproduces a transcript of the conversation, by kind permission of The Liberty Fund, and adds eight commentaries on it by distinguished scholars from around the world who are familiar with the work of Harris and Seldon. Each of them was asked to assess the 'IEA Revolution' and to comment on the Institute's influence on thinking and its challenge to government during the Harris/Seldon years.

COLIN ROBINSON
Editorial Director, Institute of Economic Affairs
Professor of Economics, University of Surrey
January 2001

FOREWORD

Over the fireplace in the boardroom at 2 Lord North Street, the very room in which this conversation takes place, hang four framed photographic portraits. Top left is 1974 Nobel Laureate F. A. Hayek and top right is the entrepreneur Antony G. A. Fisher. Below Hayek is his pupil Arthur Seldon and below Fisher is his protégé Ralph Harris. This arrangement is quite deliberate and many is the time in that room when, speaking about the IEA, I have, pointing up to all four great men and moving my finger clockwise from Hayek, said: 'Hayek advises Fisher; Fisher recruits Harris; Harris meets Seldon. In nine words, that is the start of the IEA.'

So Harris and Seldon, armed with Hayek's little blueprint *The Intellectuals and Socialism* and funded (to a small extent) and encouraged in his capacity as Chairman by Fisher, set out to replace the prevailing big government/government-is-always-right orthodoxy with a more realistic and humane market-guided vision.

Did they succeed? It is an interesting and methodologically challenging question addressed elsewhere in *The Changing Fortunes of Economic Liberalism* by David Henderson.[1]

At one level they clearly did. When I first attended IEA events

---

1   David Henderson, *The Changing Fortunes of Economic Liberalism: Yesterday, Today and Tomorrow*, London, Institute of Economic Affairs, 1998

in the 1970s its three targets were inflation, the trade unions and the nationalised industries.

Inflation in the UK has come down from all but 30 per cent p.a. to about 2.5 per cent; trade union membership has dropped from just over 50 per cent of the workforce to just under 20 per cent (and nearly 30 per cent of union members now own shares, a higher percentage than the adult population as a whole); and the once hugely subsidised nationalised industries have become for the most part world-class tax-generating entities.

At another level though, one might ask, if socialism is dead, why is government bigger? If we share Mr Blair's new-found faith in a 'dynamic market economy' why does 'tax freedom day' advance rather than retreat? Why do spending and the clamour for ever more spending grow? Why do we set new records every year for regulation?

Ralph Harris often says that in the 1950s talk of markets was akin to swearing in church (particularly when applied to labour markets), yet by 1997 the word 'socialism' did not appear in the Labour manifesto. Is James Buchanan correct when he states 'socialism is dead but Leviathan lives on'? Is Ed Feulner on to something when he asks 'Can you win the war of ideas but fail to change policy?' Trust of government surely has changed during the years that unfold in this conversation. In 1964, Feulner reports, 75 per cent trusted big government. By 1998, exactly a generation later, 75 per cent did *not* trust big government. Is the Iron Triangle of bureaucrats, politicians and interest groups unbreakable or am I being too impatient as it rusts?

While it is hard to agree on the exact scale of change – and, as the dragons of inflation, trade unionism and nationalism were slain, so those of regulation, environmentalism and others promptly emerged – we can surely agree that the market approach is today in better shape than fifty years ago and that our two conversationalists, Harris and Seldon, were key movers and shakers in the process.

Having agreed that something of significance certainly happened, the interesting question then is how did it come about? What can we learn from the experiences of these two men so that they may guide us in this new century as we face new challenges? I list below the twelve most important lessons I learned from Ralph and Arthur in this 'conversation' and I urge you not only to read the full text closely but also to savour the commentaries which follow from a group of very distinguished thinkers from the UK and around the world.

1 Packaging your message

Because both Harris and Seldon sprang from working-class roots, they did not share the then common belief that such people 'could not do all the necessary things' (AS) to provide for themselves and improve their lot. This 'armed [them] against undue sentimentality' (RH), but it did mean 'it took us ten or fifteen years to make a mark because we started off appearing to be insensitive to the lowly' (AS).

2 Public choice and history: a blend

'They [the politicians] forgot all the history of the working classes' (AS). This is the very Hayekian point about the importance of history. It is the nationalisation of health and education and welfare (AS). It is the imposition of 'a common standard', compulsory rather than voluntary contributions 'and let the politicians for electoral purposes determine the benefits' (RH). It is the evil of public choice economics when political government replaced and destroyed individual and family choice (AS).

3 Inflation

'Inflation [is] the enemy of self provision' (RH) and in turn allows the government in to take over supposedly failed private provision.

4 Product development

Determining 'what kind of book is useful' (RH), 'a reading list' with 'footnotes to encourage the students to pursue the matters discussed in more detail' plus 'lively' presentation, accessibility and 'a good read' of 'about ten thousand words' (AS).

5 Patience

It 'took us five or ten years to win the confidence of some respected journalists' (AS).

6 Popularise

'Both of us were able to popularise, write in simple language, simple English, the arguments of our authors' (AS). 'No jargon or complexities to keep the everyday reader at bay' (RH).

7 Challenging scholars

A challenge to scholars: 'Stick to your last and tell us what you think your reasoning leads to' (AS).

8 Politically impossible

'We refused to limit ourselves to what government said they could do without risking votes and all that sort of stuff'(AS).

9 Shock tactics

'A lot of our thinking was deliberately intended to affront [the establishment] and wake them up' (RH).

10 Secrets of success

Three ingredients for success: 'academic something, business something and finance' (RH). Plus 'we had faith that knowledge would work' (AS).

11 Living with yourself

'If you feel you are right, you go on arguing until you are established as having told the truth. You can't live with the untruth if you feel you have found the truth' (AS).

12 Independence

Seeing people, great public figures in the House of Lords, not free to say what they want and voting even against things they actually believe in bring to 'my mind this enormous gratitude to have had what Antony Fisher called "an independent station"' (RH).

As always, the views expressed in Occasional Paper 116 are those of the authors, not the Institute (which has no corporate view), its Managing Trustees, Academic Advisory Council Members or senior staff.

JOHN BLUNDELL
General Director
Institute of Economic Affairs
January 2001

THE THEME OF THE CONVERSATION

For some it might seem that there could hardly be a less likely starting point for two leading proponents of free-market economics than the working-class neighbourhoods of Tottenham and the East End of London. Yet it was here that two youths of the 1920s and early 1930s were learning at first hand many of the lessons that would later inspire their life's work – work that would ultimately serve as an influence on political and social events in Great Britain and around the world.

Ralph Harris and Arthur Seldon both grew up in working-class London neighbourhoods and developed a profound interest in the fundamental ideas and institutions of a free society, with particular regard to the role of markets in solving both economic and social problems. They pursued this interest through the study of economics and both were influenced early on by the work of Austrian economist and Nobel Laureate Friedrich von Hayek.

Ralph Harris was a political Conservative in his early years, and twice stood as a parliamentary candidate for the Conservative party. Arthur Seldon, like many others who had grown up in London's East End during the Depression, was a socialist in his early days. But he came to embrace classical liberal ideas whilst studying at the London School of Economics, where his main instructors included Hayek.

Both Harris and Seldon entered the world as academics: Harris as a lecturer in Economics at St Andrews University, and Seldon as a research assistant at the London School of Economics and later as tutor and staff examiner. But their interests were later drawn in another direction.

In the mid 1950s Harris departed his post in the academic world and Seldon later left his position as an economic adviser in British industry to begin work with Antony Fisher. Fisher was a man with a vision of creating an organisation dedicated to research into the role of free markets and individual liberty in solving social problems. Fisher's vision of a free-market think tank was in part influenced by his contact with Hayek.

In 1956 Fisher recruited Ralph Harris to become the general director of a fledgling organisation, the Institute of Economic Affairs or IEA. And in 1957 Arthur Seldon joined Harris and became the IEA's editorial director.

Together Harris and Seldon ran the IEA well into the 1980s. They soon began co-writing a number of publications that gave voice to what were at the time rarely heard views of economic reform based on free-market principles.

Over the next thirty years, their work, as well as the ever-expanding work of the Institute of Economic Affairs, had an enormous influence on governments, public policy and economic thought, including a profound impact on one Margaret Thatcher, who had been paying special attention to the insights of the IEA since she first met Harris and Seldon in the 1960s. Indeed many of the policies enacted by Mrs Thatcher during her ten years as Prime Minister were the direct result of work being done at the IEA.

As the IEA became the model for dozens of organisations like it around the world, the contribution to classical liberalism made by Harris and Seldon began to be fully recognised. Ralph Harris was made a life peer, and now sits in the House of Lords as Lord Harris of High Cross. Arthur Seldon was given the title of Commander of the Order of the British Empire, one of the highest honours awarded to a citizen of the United Kingdom. Both Harris and Seldon continue to serve as Founders of the still vital Institute of Economic Affairs, and both continue to work, through their speaking and writing, toward a freer society.

STEPHEN ERICKSON
E. Wilson Lyon Professor of the Humanities and Professor of Philosophy
Pomona College, Claremont, California

'Governments in search of advice looked to think tanks such as the Institute of Economic Affairs in Britain and the Heritage Foundation in the United States rather than to Oxford or Harvard.'
The Economist, December 1993

THE CONVERSATION

SE – *Professor Stephen Erickson*

RH – *Ralph Harris (Lord Harris of High Cross)*

AS – *Dr Arthur Seldon CBE*

SE: I was reading recently that Antony Fisher, who founded the IEA, was once told that he had hired the last and only two free market economists in all England. Is that the way it seemed to you?

RH: The whole opinion in those days was statist. It was post war when the IEA started in 1957. There was a socialist government. Then there was a Tory government with a large chunk of socialism built into a consensus. So economists didn't typically challenge it. They assumed it was the way that things were and that you had to rearrange the deckchairs on the *Titanic*. You had to offer little bits of advice but nothing very radical. So here were a couple of reckless, irresponsible, full-frontal market economists.

SE: At the time, did you find it difficult to find an audience?

AS: No and yes. The young were naturally left-wing. They seemed to have more compassion about people with low income. I found in my days that I was thought to be rather hard-hearted. I wasn't conscious of the suffering of the poor and so on. It took some time before you had to say things which won the confidence of the students. Nine tenths of them, I think, were left wing in the 1950s. I go back to the 1930s, when it was even worse. By the 1950s the kind of thinking that Ralph and I were beginning to use and spread was beginning to be heard. Its impact was rather slow. It took us ten or fifteen years to make a mark because we started off by appearing to be insensitive to the lowly.

RH: Let's dwell on that, Arthur, because half the battle is a battle of intentions. It's like the goodies and the baddies, and the display of compassion and concern and all that is the stock-in-trade of all politicians, particularly on the left. My belief is that we were armed against undue sentimentality at that time because we sprang from working-class families. There is no kidding about that; but the idea that the whole of the working-class population were incapable of running their own affairs and making their own decisions was offensive to us. It was a kind of affront to have the paternalistic Tories or Socialists saying that we know best and that we can guide the workers or the labouring classes or whatever you like to call them. So we were rather sharp about that and paraded our working-class confidence.

AS: I was appalled by the insensitivity of governments to the efforts of the working classes to help themselves – the belief that they could not do all the necessary things. They were most anxious to ensure that they used all the opportunities of insurance to safeguard their families in times of sickness and loss of work. I began to sense a sort of anti-working-class sentiment in all political parties. They wanted the state to do these things. They didn't like people to do things for themselves. They thought that ordinary people weren't capable. They forgot all the history of the working classes. The records are that the working classes were sending their children to school by the 1860s. They were insuring for health cover and so on by 1910–11 when all parties in England, the main ones Tory and Liberal, with people like Lloyd George and Churchill and Beveridge at the centre, passed the infamous Act of 1911 which forced the working classes to insure with the state despite the fact that nine-tenths of them were already covered by private systems. Politicians seemed to me to be saying you are not capable, you need us to ensure that you take care of your families, which was nonsense. The working classes were taking care of themselves.

SE: Did you have a similar experience, Ralph?

RH: Arthur said they ignored history. The paradox is that the trade unions had been a major instrument of mutual aid. The unions coming through after the 1850s to 1860s developed philanthropic services: labour exchanges were ways of getting unemployed chaps in their trade into jobs, they developed old-age benefits, they actually developed insurance schemes. And when the government in 1911, as Arthur said, produced these state schemes of insurance, they used the actuarial calculations of some of the better trade unions to base their contributions and benefits on. So it was all a matter of impatience, that you couldn't wait for this to develop in a voluntary way, and a spontaneous natural way, as Hayek would say. You had to enforce a common standard system on everybody and compel contributions and let the politicians for electoral purposes determine the benefits.

SE: Arthur, were there events in your personal life that drew you to your thinking?

AS: Yes, there was one, early on. When I was nine or ten, my foster-father died, and I learned from that event that he had covered his wife and me by an insurance. Within two days, the secretary of the Friendly Society which had covered us came with a huge cheque, for £100, which would look after us for two or three years. That taught me that if one man is doing it, others were doing it too. And from then I learned that, far from government having to do such things, the ordinary people were learning because of their consciousness of their own selves, of their wives, dependants, and so on. And from that, I think, I must have learned the early beginning of my suspicion that government was doing far too much, and that it should leave people, even if they did come from below, to do things for themselves.

SE: Do you have a similar sort of experience, Ralph?

RH: When my mother died, I found in a shoebox four policies. She had four children, and I found four policies taken out on our births for funeral benefit. The working class feared that they wouldn't have the money to bury their dead, so you could take out for a penny or halfpenny a week an insurance policy to pay five pounds on the death of any of these children; four children, four policies, sixpence a week altogether and five pounds on it. That was the prudence of the best kind of working class. But when my mother died the five pounds wasn't worth a bean because of inflation, the enemy of self provision. If you insured, you put money on the shelf for a rainy day and then inflation would render it almost worthless. And the government would have to come in. That was one of the reasons that led things more and more into the public sector.

SE: If I remember, in 1949 Antony Fisher heard you give a talk in Sussex, and he told you that he was going to put the money together and start an institute. But it was seven years before that happened?

RH: Yes. I kept in touch with Antony. I had been working at the University of St Andrews in Scotland, and I came down a couple of times a year and met Antony occasionally. The great thing about Antony Fisher is that he was a non-conformist. He had been at Eton, he was a country gentleman, he had an extensive farm and all of that, but he had this bee in his bonnet that the war had been fought (he had been in the air force) over freedom and individual self-expression, and increasingly the state seemed to be closing in on people from all parties. So to me Antony was a breath of fresh air, and when he got a bit of cash and said 'Look, we are ready to go and start up this institute we talked about,' almost recklessly we threw ourselves into it, first me, then Arthur soon after.

AS: Well, Ralph, there had never been anything like this before. The academics, mostly on the left, the mild left, who thought the government ought to expand itself and so on, were mostly sympathisers with left-wing thought. We were the only people, it seemed, at the time to think something that was revolutionary. We had the nerve to say that all the thinking that was being done by these well-meaning young men was wrong, that they were working on fallacies and we would challenge them. Somehow that was a revolutionary thing to have said, even before we had published our first works.

SE: You quickly developed a publishing arm, and very quickly sought out people who would write for you, is that right?

AS: Even at that time, people of adequate quality to write the kinds of works that we had in mind were so scarce that Ralph and I had to join together and write three of the main works ourselves in 1958/9 and 1960. Those were the ones we wrote on hire-purchase credit. We also wrote books which made their mark on advertising, which was universally scorned as wasteful, taught wrong values, and so on.

SE: You did pensions.

AS: I did pensions myself. Then we started a series of surveys from 1964 into the supposed view that all the people were happy to pay higher taxes in order that the government could spend more on schools, health services and so on. From our learning of economic thought, we had a doubt about all of that, and the reason was that all the surveys being done simply asked, 'Would you pay more tax if the government spent more on schooling and health services and pensions and other things?' We found if you introduced the notion that there was another way of financing welfare services, and that was by payment (charging fees and so on), that standards of quality would rise. We did that work over something like ten years or more, and that began to show the evidence. We found that people said, 'In that case I won't pay higher taxes: I will pay by prices.' And that helped us on our way to show that there were other ways of supplying.

SE: Whom did you try to reach? Who was your target audience?

RH: I will tell you, this is where financing came in. We hadn't the money to set up a major publishing effort, produce books for everyman, get into the bookshops and build up a sales force and all the rest of it. We had to think, how do we, with a few thousand pounds a year, make any impression? And so our target was frankly journalists, writers on good papers, the *Financial Times*, *The Times*, the *Guardian*, because if they would review our books, they would multiply the effect, and the books themselves were devised accordingly. Arthur and I sat down and thought, as students, what kind of book is useful? About ten thousand words, Arthur decided was a good read, about forty or fifty pages. The book would have to have a reading list for further reading for students. The book would have to have footnotes to encourage the students to pursue the matters discussed in more detail if they wished. They had to be presented in a lively form and they had to be well written: accessible to a good sixth former, the highest grade in secondary school, or first-year undergraduates.

SE: Were the journalists easy to reach? Were they accessible? Did they want to read what you wrote?

AS: At first, no. At first they were very doubtful about these two odd guys who were saying something that no one had said in this kind of way. And it took us five or ten years to win the confidence of some respected journalists.

SE: How did you interest them?

AS: By sending them copies. They were invited to launches. In this very room.

RH: Launches and lunches. Journalists like lunches with a drink and snacks.

AS: After five years or so, we managed to find new authors and young men who had heard of us and were thinking along the lines that we were working on. And they were beginning to have some doubt about whether it was necessary, or a good thing, for government to go on expanding its realm.

SE: How long was it before you were paid enough attention to be attacked in the press? Did that come?

AS: I think not much notice of us was taken by government people until 1966, when a minister quoted a paper of ours that argued that the so-called National Plan of the government was going to lapse or fail. We then began to feel that if we managed to get our work known by people in office they would take us more seriously than they seemed to be doing in the early years. And from about the mid 1960s I would say that we had a feeling that we were at last being heard. But that was a full ten years after we started.

RH: That was the Labour government that came into power in 1964. In 1965 it put out a circular or questionnaire to all of industry and business asking them how much timber they would need, how much labour they would need, how much exports. This was totally preposterous. We published a paper by a lapsed socialist, John Brunner, called *The National Plan*, predicting before the plan was published that it would be a failure because you couldn't operate these macro magnitudes, you had no leverage to influence building, exports, manufacturing. The National Plan collapsed in nine months.

SE: As you can imagine, we do a little background study before these interviews, and find out dark strange things. In your case, Arthur, I don't know if I have wrong information, but once upon a time you were a socialist?

AS: Oh yes, and it was easy to be one. You see, I lived with people whose incomes were low and whose living standards were low too. And it seemed to me at the age of sixteen, perhaps a bit more than that, seventeen, that it was logical, as the socialists then said and taught, that government would have to do more, to give people money, to give them free services. The welfare state was in its infancy in a sense, and it seemed to me with my young mind that untypically accepted the dominant view, that it would be up to the government, and especially a Labour government, because they seemed to be saying more about what the workers ought to be given and so on. So it was natural for big-hearted, generous-hearted young people to think that it was the Labour Party which would do this.

SE: What made it hard for you to stay a socialist? Was there one particular event that was a watershed for you, or was it a gradual process?

AS: My illusions were dropped when I went to the London School of Economics as a student. Most economics teachers were of the Hayekian type. Hayek lectured to me from 1934 when I was eighteen, and from then I abandoned my illusion that only government could supply all the things that the people needed. And I began to switch from the view that the state was essential, to saying that it was not supplying services in a way that best suited the diverse circumstances of the workers.

SE: Was it Hayek's views that inspired the two of you most, Ralph?

RH: Well, for me it would be Hayek that I'd go back to again and again for real inspiration. At this point, would you hand me the big book? This is something of a Bible for me. It's the *Constitution of Liberty*, published in 1960, just after the IEA started, and it has a marvellous final chapter, called 'Why I am not a Conservative'. This is the passage that I like to repeat to students:

> The main merit of the individualism which Adam Smith and his contemporaries advocated, is that it is a system under which bad men can do least harm. It is a social system which does not depend for its functioning on our finding good men for running it, or all men becoming better than they now are, but which makes use of men in all their given variety and complexities, sometimes good, sometimes bad, sometimes intelligent, more often stupid.

That is his defence for the free society.

SE: I would like to talk a little about the way the two of you relate now. Yours is a very long-term relationship, and I gather it must be one of the more interesting relationships in your lives?

AS: I spent most of my working life with this man for thirty years, and we bounce off each other. He always made me think harder about some things I was teaching and thinking at the time. I suppose unless there was a basic sympathy of outlook and hope it would have been difficult for two men to have lived and worked together in sympathy, with the occasional difference of emphasis, not difference of thought as it were, but difference of emphasis. He would say, 'No, no, that's going too fast.' And I used to say, 'Well, that's going too slow, the thing is happening faster than you think.'

RH: We had adjoining rooms and they had folding doors mostly left open, so that we were calling through to one another. I can't think of anyone else in my wide acquaintance that I could conceivably have worked with, not for years, let alone thirty years, in that close proximity and have as few frictions as Arthur and I developed. It was partly for me this working-class bond. I didn't want to become a militant working-class lad, but I admired Arthur and his background in the East End of London and that he was an adopted son, and the aspirations that he had for other working-class people. I felt no less proud of my own working-class origins. I had a bit of a chip on my shoulder. If I met public-school boys I would mock their county accents, because these were the people who would condescend to help workers along with little state hand-outs and subsidies and benefits.

SE: I gather you divided up responsibilities, and you, Arthur, were mostly involved in publishing?

AS: After the early years – when we had passed the first five years or so, during which it was difficult to get authors of the right calibre. So some things we did jointly. After that, the great virtue and value of Ralph for me, for my personal mission in life, which was to get the ideas over, was that he was a past master at selling, at persuading and explaining and so on, with audiences of students, businessmen and journalists. And of course he raised money, from about the mid 1960s onwards, I think. And so I found my salesman as it were. He may have found his backroom boy. As the saying goes, I ran the engine room.

RH: I kept the shop! How much is just pure chance and happy accident? But we had a complete division of labour. I would consult Arthur about financial matters and all of that, and he would always let me see manuscripts and even proofs. But he was publications. He said, 'Look, Ralph, I run better on a loose rein.' And I learned not to try and breathe down his neck too fiercely. On the other hand, he was happy for me to raise money. The only arguments we ever had were: 'Why don't we spend more on publicity? Why not more on marketing?' And it was a good point. If we had had unlimited money, we could have saturated the market with some of our writings much more quickly than we did.

SE: I gather early on there was an important need to be provocative in what you wrote and said in order to gather some further attention? Was this a kind of cultural strategy?

AS: One of Ralph's virtues was that he could write well. He wrote leaders for the *Glasgow Herald*, which meant he wrote well. Whatever he said, he wrote well. I also managed to work up a sort of column as well in the *Telegraph*, which was the first national paper that began to see what our aim was. So both of us were able to popularise, write in simple language, simple English, the arguments of our authors.

RH: The division of labour was . . . I mean Arthur was an ace editor, who has always written lucidly and clearly, in simple, direct, accessible English, with no jargon or complexities to keep the everyday reader at bay. Our authors relied upon Arthur's editing. Hayek said the best thing he ever published was by the IEA: Arthur had taken a manuscript and done as he wished with that publication. 'The best thing I ever wrote,' said Hayek. So Arthur was perfecting these things; I was the old journalist manqué: thinking of slogans, phrases. We had these excitable titles like 'The Price of Blood', 'Anything but Action'.

AS: 'Down with the Poor'.

RH: 'Down with the Poor'.

SE: Since you were a charity, was there a little bit of a worry that you might dangerously get identified with one particular party or another?

AS: Not often, because we knew that we could easily substantiate our . . .

RH: Scholarly? . . .

AS: . . . rectitude. We were searchers after the truth, and the papers on the left, which had adverse thoughts that we were right-wing and so on, quite soon accepted that we were raising serious questions which they had ignored in much of their work.

RH: This was the strange thing – Arthur would always make it very clear in his prefaces. He wrote these masterly prefaces to every study, and he would specify our approach was to examine the ways in which markets could better serve consumer preferences that are changing, and progressing in dynamic society, and so forth. And he spelled all that out: in other words, the basic principles of a market economy. They were regarded as very tendentious by some socialists. People like Wedgwood Benn still think the market economy is the work of the devil. So the paradox is that the very fundamental assumptions that we had specified, drawing on our great mentors, Adam Smith and Hume, and all the other thinkers like Hayek, are now almost universally accepted in adult society. Tony Blair ran for leadership of the Labour Party on the basis of a 'dynamic market economy' – that was his phrase, 'a dynamic market economy'. Inconceivable that anyone before Mrs Thatcher would use those words, inconceivable that even Margaret Thatcher would have said 'a dynamic market economy'.

AS: There is more to it, though. I found when we started to make use of young university economists that they were limiting themselves to saying 'My analysis shows that government should do A, B and C. There is no point in my discussing D, E and F. I understand that the government would not tackle them. It would be too difficult.' So I said, 'We are hiring you as a scholar, not as a forecaster, just keep to your . . .' – what's the word?

RH: Stick to your last.

AS: Stick to your last and tell us what you think your reasoning leads to. What are the things that the government ought to do if your reasoning is well founded? Re-introduce the things that you think would or would not do, and tell us what the government ought to do. That apparently shocked them at first, because they said, 'We won't get anywhere, we won't reach a higher status if we go on to say what government can't do. So we are just going to say what government can do.' But in time they learned that in the long run they were going to be more highly regarded as academics who were doing their life's work in explaining the initially unpopular things which their analysis had led to. There was also Hayek who came on the scene and wrote that the job of scholars is to make possible what seems to the government impossible and that was really one way of describing the Institute's work: that we refused to limit ourselves to what government said they could do without risking votes and all that sort of stuff.

RH: This thing about 'politically impossible'. There is an amazing passage that I have gone back to time after time, from Hayek's *The Intellectuals and Socialism,* which was first published in 1949 by the Institute of Humane Studies. Listen to this:

> The main lesson which the true liberal must learn from the success of the Socialists, is that it was their courage to be utopian, which gave them the support of the intellectual, and therefore an influence on public opinion, which is daily making possible that which only recently seemed utterly remote.

Ignore received wisdom completely ('political correctness', we now say) about what can be done. Say what you think should be done. That is what Hayek did and was widely mocked for in the earlier days. And that is what our authors, under Arthur's prodding, increasingly did.

AS: The great debt that academics owe society is to speak the truth, even if it's untimely and awkward, and even if it risks their jobs.

RH: You see, there was a sense really in which Arthur and I relished that; we were like cheeky schoolboys. I mean, we had come from nowhere and didn't know where we were going, and so liked the idea of throwing a little cracker down at their feet. So, you see, a lot of our thinking was deliberately intended to affront them and wake them up. I think we enjoyed it and it was a necessary part of this Hayekian challenge.

SE: Were there any special early successes that you really relished, that gave you a sense that yes, it is beginning to work and work well, that you are progressing?

AS: Denis Lees, who got his chair a number of years after he worked for us, had written a short piece in *The Times* saying that the desirable range of health services would never be established out of taxes, and that before long (and this was 1962) the nation and all parties and all schools of thought would have to consider other sources of revenue. He did well out of that; it made him famous.

RH: There were lots of comments . . .

AS: There were lots of comments on that: he was right, he was wrong, he was half right, he was half wrong, but we made news.

RH: Lees did a Hobart Paper called *Health Through Choice*, which presented the classic contrast between a developing, ingenious, innovative, private, free-range scheme, and this stark state monopoly that we still have. He became a professor quite soon after that. By the way, we paid these authors peanuts. We hadn't much money anyway, and in the early stages we chose younger economists and we paid them a hundred guineas. That was £105. And that was all. No expenses and trips or treats. And gradually we had queues of people wanting to write Hobart Papers, genuinely because they thought it was a way of making progress, of getting attention, and making their way.

AS: We asked them to be unconventional, unorthodox and daring in the analysis of the subject on which they had worked. And we told them to persevere, even if their conclusions were unwelcome, were awkward or wouldn't suit the establishment. One man (well, two men) wrote the case for charging for blood. Hell broke loose! Wicked, unkind, but there was a man who nearly lost his life because there was a shortage of his blood, a rare group. It took some time to find, and he was saved. But this man asked the surgeon, 'How is it you are short of blood?' and he said, 'Oh well, we don't want to charge for something as important as blood: we think that people ought to give it, and they are giving it free.' I said, 'Would you rather . . .' – sorry, the patient said, 'Would you rather I'd have died than charge?' 'Oh,' he said, 'that's a difficult question.'

SE: Here is something that is referred to by some as your intellectual debut. This would be 1959, when you hosted the Mont Pèlerin Society meeting. I believe it was at Christchurch, Oxford, and very notable people came to those meetings. What was it like going into those meetings? Did you get any stage fright?

AS: We were invited by Professor John Jewkes, at Oxford, to write a paper on the subject of advertising, based on one of the books we had worked on at the time, the economics of advertising, which was a hate word. The whole of the left wing thought that advertising was just a waste indulged in by capitalists to make people buy their goods. It was feasible, it was plausible, to an extent. But devising the programme was Jewkes's job, and he asked us to do a paper. The conference was attended by Hayek and the other economists who had founded the MPS twelve years earlier. It was the first time we had been invited to give a paper. At the conference, Milton Friedman and George Stigler came up to me. I didn't know them very well: one was enormously tall, the other rather short, and they said, 'Hello, we are Friedman and Stigler,' and I said, appallingly, 'So what?' In a sort of friendly voice, but at the time neither of us knew too much of their work. The point was that that one book on advertising made us known to the world of academics, teaching the kind of doctrines that we thought ought to have been more widely known.

RH: Bear in mind in 1959 there was Galbraith in full spate in the United States and there was Packard and others, on 'the throwaway society'. It was all meant to be an attack on the advertiser, but it really amounted to an attack upon the consumer. The consumer was a victim, he couldn't defend himself, he took anything that was told to him, and so on, and Stigler had produced this great joke that I enjoyed, which was that it was like blaming the waiter in a restaurant for your own obesity (he had made you fat), instead of blaming yourself for overeating. The consumer was always in charge, and advertising was one of the activities going on all the time, in the press, in debates, in politics, in trying to argue for ideas for products, for services. The idea that advertising was uniquely powerful, or that it was uniquely wasteful, or a complete distortion of the whole market system was one that we had to combat not only in the Labour government. Tories too, high Tories, said, 'Oh, I don't like all this advertising and letting the working class get sight of the things that give them ideas above their station.' There was press advertising and we had just had television advertising. So really it was quite time we took that as a very serious threat to our whole belief in free choice.

AS: But academically, Ralph, the whole world of academics who were thinking like us, or were beginning to think like us, did see that conference paper and the book as establishing the moral right for us to be accepted as new young men who were beginning to spread the right doctrines.

SE: You hosted the Mont Pèlerin Society meetings in 1959. Was there a strategy behind that? Something you hoped to accomplish?

RH: It came to us as a bit of a surprise, and a distraction. We had only got going a couple of years earlier, and suddenly we had an Oxford conference, and all the arrangements about guests and hotel rooms, and lunches and translations. We had to get translations at those early meetings, so it was totally unwelcome as far as I was concerned. I also knew we had to pay some money towards it, so it was more unwelcome for me. But Arthur exploited the Mont Pèlerin Society and got a good return.

AS: We found by the middle 1960s and 1970s the think tanks (which is a word that must now be used) were being formed in other countries, like the Fraser Institute in Canada, and they were beginning to arrange and model their work more or less on our lines. And it was they, after some time, who also produced younger men, and women too, who we could draw on as authors.

SE: Did they get their idea of forming themselves from observing your IEA activities?

AS: There is a view voiced here and there, that there are now something like sixty or a hundred institutes which to some extent are replicas almost of us and the work we did. I would say that it is true, that most of them did learn our methods, and they certainly picked up the underlying philosophic thinking that we had used and applied.

RH: Well, this is a good opportunity to come back to the IEA and its foundation, and the relationship between Arthur and me, and Antony Fisher. I came to be secretary of the Mont Pèlerin Society in about 1965, after the Oxford conference. For ten years I was secretary, arranging these meetings around the world. In those days they were very cheap; obviously it was student accommodation for most of the people who attended, and the programmes were the same as they had always been, the fundamental principles of the free society. But when after that we began to go around a lot of countries, Fisher and I went round Europe. We went to Germany, to France, to Spain, to Italy, to Switzerland, to try and create an IEA, not as a sub-office of ours – we didn't want anything to do with it – but to bring people together. We could find academics, but we couldn't find people like me who would reliably dig their heels in and get an office and money going. There were no entrepreneurs. Whereas there is a tradition here of businesses supporting education, university and academic things, there doesn't seem to be that kind of tradition elsewhere. All that is interesting to me because Fisher, who we usually take for granted putting up the original money, provided the entrepreneurial capital backing for us two to have our heads.

AS: The thing that surprised me was that we had no similar institutes here in England. The first new effort to copy our work or to learn from it came in 1975, eighteen years after we began here.

RH: The Adam Smith Institute.

AS: Absolutely. Since then there are another three or more, established mostly in the mid 1970s. Overseas also it surprised me that it seemed to take a fair time before someone said, 'Look, we ought to have an IEA here', wherever 'here' was. And that I can't explain.

RH: I have explained it. Forgive me, I have explained it. The particular ingredient you require is academic something, business something and finance, and you would get one or even two of these, but not three.

AS: Once we started we needed some years in order to make our work widely known and accepted, and then it was easier, I think, to raise funds. Once we received the money that some firms had started to give us, we began to influence opinions. Once *The Times* and the *Telegraph* and other papers began to say, 'These people are talking sense, why have we ignored them for all these years?', that was the thing that induced a number of donors to say, 'Well, let's give them X.'

SE: What makes it sound so courageous, even daring, is that no one would have known at the time – you might, so to speak, have been out on the streets without a job in 1960 because things didn't work out.

AS: The answer?

SE: Yes.

AS: Faith that we were right: faith that the thinking that had been understated, ignored and so on by academia would re-establish itself. And if we could risk some years of our lives – and our wives in a sense – then we would get there in the end. It was an act of faith.

RH: I have a difference with Arthur. Arthur said we were borne up by faith and so forth. I would just amend that a tiny bit. Provisionally, tentatively, it was knowledge. Once I had read Hayek's writings, I saw that it was inconceivable that an efficient economy could ever be established based upon central direction, because in Hayek's more elaborate formulation, you could never collect enough knowledge at the centre to reach out and indicate to all of the independent actors around the economy what they should do about investment, production, export and importing and all that. We know that the market economy is necessary to bring together this information. An information-sharing system, that is the market economy. I mean we really did have more than faith. We had this knowledge.

AS: So the sequence was: We had faith that knowledge would work.

RH: Ah, well done! We had faith that knowledge would work.

SE: One thing is clear: ideas have really mattered to you. Which were the ideas that drove you as you began your work together?

AS: With me, the idea was that only in open markets would people realise the maximum merits of their faculties. It's only in markets in the long run that people will do themselves good, do good for themselves and their families or their causes, the church: only by doing good to others, because others will gain from the activities that they offer, or services or advice or whatever it is they offer. It's only if they benefit others that they will do good for themselves and their causes. That's the moral justification of markets.

SE: At that time at least, didn't many people think markets were flat out immoral?

AS: They thought the markets were solely devised for maximising your profits at the expense of the customers. That's what the left taught. It was only government which would have the impetus to do good for you by taking your money (taxes, etc.) and spending it. You would never know who the best sellers of services were until you had a choice, among a number of them. The government gives you one choice. It tells you: 'Give us your money and we will give you goods and services in which you have no choice and from which you can't escape.' That is immoral. The market says: 'Give us your money, or give to us rather than our rivals, and we will give you more than they will.' That is moral.

SE: You thought that way as well, Ralph?

RH: Yes. One of the powerful insights of Hayek is competition as a 'discovery procedure' – to discover what you are best at and how you can best help other people you need an open market, because they have to express their views, what is their notion of their destiny, their notion of self-fulfilment. In an open market you have suppliers and demanders, and you find out the best way of producing something, the best way of distributing something, the best way of packaging it and making . . . by copying lots of different people, appealing to the sovereign consumer. In our system, the consumer was the boss, it was consumer preference that determined the whole shape of the economy. So that to me it was a matter of self-respect, and my respect for other people, by not telling them what is good for them or how they should comport themselves. I may have arguments and discussions and express my view. But in the end, real morality is free conduct; it's what people do with themselves, not what you make them do at gunpoint.

SE: Yes, but you are saying that governments aren't even honest competitors in the market.

AS: No. The government says, 'Give us your taxes, and we will give you services in which you have no choice.'

RH: What is good for you – what they think is good for you.

AS: 'We are the one supplier. If you give us your money, we the government are the only supplier of goods and services.' So you are caught. 'We are the sole supplier of the things that we think you ought to have. We can fool you into giving us part of your income, and we will give you services which we control, and you have no escape.' Government is not run by the people, it's run by the bosses, the bosses who can organise and activate and influence. This notion of government has made prisoners of us all.

RH: Alas, you need government, but big government is subject to such flaws, incorrigible flaws. Big government is irresponsible government because they can't know all the circumstances of the nation, the society, the families that they are administering. Big government leads to all kinds of deals, backstage deals about policies, and all the time they are governed not by the public interest, but by the self-interest of the politicians to maintain their power. You need politicians, but the more you can contain politicians to the central tasks they have to do, the less you tempt them into this vote-grabbing, this corruption and deceit which is inseparable from modern, mass, undiscriminating democratic politics.

AS: Government starts too soon. It doesn't wait to see if markets can supply something but better. Once it's in, it goes much too far. It does more things than it was authorised to do by the voters. And not least, once it's in, it stays too long. The welfare state goes on and on, whatever the circumstances. It is impossible to make government accept the logic of their function, that at the most they have been called for a short time, to do little, and get the hell out of it. But they don't, and this is the lesson. This lesson we have yet to learn.

RH: Arthur and I both had experience of living through the Second World War, a nation at war. I was still at school when the war broke out and Arthur had just left the London School of Economics. One of the real legends about the war was the 'Dunkirk spirit', that when Britain stood alone against the embattled forces of Hitler on the continent, the Channel was there and we expected our few hundred thousand remaining soldiers to be brought back to our island and we were all united. In the Dunkirk spirit, we stood together and we bent our shoulders to the wheel and all that. Again and again in the late 1940s and the 1950s, politicians for their own purpose conjured up the Dunkirk spirit. Things were difficult, they were a shambles, devaluation . . . we need the Dunkirk spirit, they said, we need it to recreate the unity of war. It is essentially a totalitarian concept. It is like conscripting the whole nation again in peace. When that kind of thing was happening outside and we were watching, we didn't talk about the principles of it. It was a monstrous assault upon the fundamental freedom of every man, woman and child.

SE: Now some say that by the 1960s the Tories had run out of ideas and their having run out of ideas was a great opportunity for you, in that they came seeking ideas. What do you say to that?

AS: The first Conservative who came to us to ask for our view did so, I think, in 1964 when they lost power. Keith Joseph came with a colleague who I remember had lost a leg in the war. He said, 'We are told we should know what you are up to and the ideas you have been working on.' This was the first time that any senior Conservative came to ask us what we were doing. He felt he should know. The next thing was silence for ten years until he came again in 1974 when Heath lost. Then he was more interested. Things were more dangerous. The Conservatives had been losing far too often. And then, I would say by 1974, some of the more intelligent Tories were beginning to see the ideas that they had peddled and won power on since the war were outdated.

SE: Arthur, you have written that cash gives choice and dignity, whereas welfare systems enslave. Could you say something more about that?

AS: Yes. Our welfare state gives to the poor, the sick, the halt, the lame and the blind. It gives them goods and services, which means treating them like children who have no power to choose or make or have a view. You treat them as though they were aged eight, ten or twelve. They have no choice. You give them a comfort which may work for some time, but you deny them the power, the sense that people have the power, to make a choice, and to say, 'I would like to try this first before I see which is as good, worse or better.' A welfare state that was sensitive to the feelings of people being helped would say you can have either cash or kind, and you take the risk. We think that if you have cash you will in time learn where to get the best schools, doctors, homes and so on and so on. But it is a symptom, and a symptomatic weakness, of all governments that we have lived under, that they prefer to give goods and services.

RH: But that's the essence of the state. That is the essence of the welfare state, that is paternalism. That is to say, you do treat people as children and you go on treating them as children. One of my favourite quotes is from Nassau Senior in the nineteenth century, who justified state education as a preliminary first step of spreading education amongst young people, so that at some stage, he said towards the last quarter of the twentieth century, people will have learned the value of education and would wish to pay for it themselves. Now we have had a century of compulsory, universal state-provided education. We are constantly informed by researchers that there is a twenty per cent adult illiteracy rate, that half of the children are below their reading age, the reading skill they should have reached at that age. State education is one of the most terrible flawed failed industries or services in the whole of this nation. There is no way that a private education company could have gone on for a hundred years with a worsening output with every sign of failure, and gone on being funded and funded. Yet state education can do that.

One of the results of the welfare state, I believe, has been to fragment the family in all kinds of ways. The families in which Arthur and I were born had some sense of mutual responsibility. When my old grandmother fell ill, my mother, the only daughter, went round to the other six children, and collected a bit of money to help their mother. That was an example that came to me, and in time when my mother was rather old and frail, I managed to summon up a few shillings to help and encourage her, although she would not have wished to have it. I think the welfare state has said: 'Look, forget all that, there are entitlements, the mother can go and get the benefits at the local post office. They are handing out cash up the road.' What is the point of families sacrificing or sharing? I do really think – there are many other considerations as well, no doubt – that the welfare state has had a cruel effect on that mutuality of family, of a neighbourhood that used to help.

SE: As the 1960s progressed, not the least of your efforts involved a growing relationship with Margaret Thatcher. Tell us a little bit about that.

RH: I think Arthur was a bit more cautious about this than I was, and I suppose she must have known. I had never discussed that I had been a Tory, a 'Liberal Unionist' candidate, living in Scotland in 1955. But we really had no close relations, no particular relationship with Mrs Thatcher until the 1970s, and she didn't stand out. Anyway, the idea of a lady being a Prime Minister, or very prominent in the Tory Party, would not have struck us as being very plausible. So that it was only through Keith Joseph that we met Margaret Thatcher, and we had her here with other MPs – Labour MPs, journalists and so forth. I remember in this room, here on this carpet, introducing Margaret Thatcher to Hayek in the 1980s when she was Prime Minister. And the unkind quip I always make is that although she is known as being a rather overpowering lady, she sat down like a meek schoolgirl and listened to Hayek. And there was a period of unaccustomed silence from Margaret Thatcher. She said nothing for about ten minutes while he deployed his argument.

SE: I have heard this put two ways. One is that you were a Thatcherite before her time, and the other is there wouldn't have been Thatcherism without your ideas.

AS: In the sense that she had copied some of the things that we had argued for years and years and years, to call it by her name, it is arguable that we anticipated her. In her younger years, in the 1960s and early in the 1970s, there was little sign that she was going to act on our thinking. But certainly she is the head of government that did more in her ten years than any other since the war, and including Churchill and Lloyd George.

RH: I remember one lunch – she came each year – and I would assemble half a dozen academics, all professors, Arthur and myself, Margaret Thatcher and her parliamentary private secretary. On one occasion in the mid 1980s, we got on to this question about the welfare state, and the indispensability of some radical reform in order to provide scope for reduced taxes. This was pressed very hard, and she suddenly sat back in her chair, and said, 'Oh dear, I didn't expect to come to the IEA and be so disheartened.' I had to explain to her that that was exactly how free-range chickens were behaving and speaking. She said she didn't want to lose the next election and although 'very sure of your ideas, there is no way of doing it and carrying people with me'. Politicians are prisoners. They have become prisoners of the welfare state.

SE: And yet she did more for IEA ideas practically speaking than any other Prime Minister, is that right?

RH: The great thing that had been a feature of our teaching, by the way going back to the early days of the 1957/8 period, was the requirement to remove the legal privileges of trade unions. Trade unions in post-war Britain had become completely in charge of whole industries, the steel industry, the coal industry, the car industry, shipbuilding. And you had the constant strike threat being held over the head of the employers, and you had the availability of subsidies from the government to prop up industries that had yielded to the strike threat and had been rendered uncompetitive. So you had the government bolstering the power of trade unions to extract unjustified wage increase. There was a kind of madness. You looked and wondered how this could be sustained. Thatcher took that one head-on, and I think she made war, there is no mistake about that. To this day, even in places like the House of Lords, her name is execrated by the old trade union members of the Labour Party, because she defeated them, she took their power away – no strikes without a ballot; if you strike you may be sued for damage imposed; if you strike, you can only pursue an industrial dispute in your business, not a political dispute to support some other strike in the dockyards or somewhere else.

AS: She did more to deprive government of its powers. She did more than any other head of government to deprive it of powers that they exercised in all the post-war years until her first year. She did more to de-socialise, de-nationalise. Hers is the only government that did more than merely moderately alter the laws that governed unions' influence or power. She actually had a public quarrel that did more I think than almost anything else: it showed that the government was prepared to live up to its promises to deprive the miners of the excesses with which they had laid down the laws about their rights.

SE: There was a famous dinner in 1978, shall I say engineered or planned, and Margaret Thatcher and Milton Friedman were at that dinner.

RH: I recall the occasion when we had asked Keith Joseph, as being less busy than Thatcher, to meet Milton Friedman in a hotel he was staying at in St James's. At the last minute Keith Joseph couldn't come, and he phoned to apologise, asking would it be all right if Margaret Thatcher came instead. I thought that would be very satisfactory. Milton and particularly Rose were excited by the possibility of meeting this formidable lady. It was exactly like a seminar, with Friedman answering questions and leading her on a bit. The key point was when he said that the essential first step in bringing the British economy under the discipline of market forces was to free the exchange rate and the whole of exchange controls. Let exchange controls wither away! You couldn't take the money abroad, you couldn't invest money in dollar stocks without going through the Bank of England and bidding for a pool of money to buy as dollars for investment. All of that, he said, we should sweep away. She was shocked by this and said, 'All the money will flow out of the country. What will happen – the bank rate will go through the roof.' 'No, ma'am, no, ma'am,' he said, and he was literally explaining to her that it could strengthen the pound. If you showed the confidence to cast off these controls and regulations and say we are going to run our own house, stick to monetary control, and so forth, then people might think this is quite a good currency to hang on to. It was a classic Friedman outcome. The pound rose to $2 to the pound, it had previously been down to $1.2 and all that kind of thing. It was the first step that the Chancellor of the Exchequer took after the election. The election was in May, and that was done in September/October of that same year, 1979.

SE: Well, I have asked about the effects of Margaret Thatcher in the sense of her putting into reality or putting into effect a number of your ideas. I sense that you weren't quite as happy, Arthur, about the way that worked out as perhaps Ralph was. Did I misread you?

AS: No, she did much more than any other head of government, but there were some things on which I had worked, schools vouchers for example. These were my own special pet schemes. To me the welfare state is the worst bane on the backs of the workers. It's the thing that holds them back, they are given things instead of having the choice and so on, and I think Keith Joseph was interested and was going ahead quite well with the idea of giving the working classes money with which to pay for fees at private schools which they hadn't had before. And he was doing quite well until the last month or two when it was being considered by the cabinet. I mustn't say this, what on earth am I doing, telling cabinet secrets?

RH: He's written it, in *The Riddle of the Voucher*.

AS: Did he? It's all relevant, so he had to confess and told the House of Commons one day in 1983 that, although there was general commendation of the idea, which is a common Conservative phrase for saying 'We would love to do it but it's too damned hard', it was thought that there was not going to be a harvest of votes in the time that would make it politically profitable. So the whole idea was abandoned. I don't blame her for the things she didn't do, but what I am saying is there was a lot that she did, more than any other leader, but there were some things that some of us had worked on for a long time and in which she said she was interested – and afterwards regretted that she had not done.

SE: Let me tell you about some words said about you by your opposition and see what your reaction is to them. The Fabians said that this New Right (which is the way they labelled you at the time) thought that liberty was not possible without markets, and that liberty really mattered. And that's the way they chose to describe you, and then of course went on to say they weren't altogether sure about how true or important that was.

AS: I would say it is difficult to think of any fundamentally justifiable exceptions. Even the things that government does, it has no right to do unless it has given the market a chance to show whether it can supply better.

RH: I remember a marvellous phrase that I used on public platforms and university debates; that the collectivists (we didn't always say socialists, there were collectivists from all parties) were people who believed in free-range chickens, but not in free-range people. But there is this underlying contempt for other people and this assumption of superiority by the collectivist individual, who thinks that liberty is too good for ordinary people to use or misuse. Our great teaching from Hayek was that people grow through exercising freedom. What people are, what people actually are, is expressed by their free thoughts and their free actions, not by things they are made to do by the state.

AS: If you don't allow them their freedom to take risks, you will never know whether they have bettered themselves by subjecting themselves to the powers of government. There is no constitutional or moral justification for imprisoning people in the hands of government which has not been subject to the test that the market might have done more things better. Full stop.

RH: Liberty carries with it individual responsibilities. Responsibility for yourself, and hopefully your family and as far as possible for your neighbours. But it does throw responsibility on to our own shoulders. Well, that is what living means, it doesn't mean shrugging off responsibility and taking soft options. It actually means embracing opportunities and also risking difficulties.

SE: Let me move to something that moves up all of this into the twenty-first century. There seems to be a great deal of political integration that is occurring now, and also a significant amount of economic integration that's occurring as well, not just in Europe but in some ways throughout the world. I guess that has to do with the way markets are becoming globalised. What do you think the effects of that are going to be on human liberty?

RH: In some ways all of these – information technology, globalisation, freer travel – are an enormous enlargement of liberty. By the way, in all my general speeches on this kind of topic I simply refer to a truism, that whatever the future holds, whatever uncertainties befall, all we can say is that our own responses and our institutions should be as flexible as possible to absorb shocks, and not rigid and fixed, like the planners would have us. The planners would have us with a plan, with a scheme, a national project. All of that is at risk in a globalised world. So we want freer markets, I mean really freer markets, freer labour markets as well as freer product markets, and I worry that we don't have that in Europe.

SE: Do you agree with that, Arthur?

AS: I agree with the general direction of it. I think it's a question of weighing up the impact that this will have on the power of governments to rule in the areas where they have sovereignty. I think that the technological changes of the past ten or fifteen years centred on the internet, and the freedom it gives to people in Asia and Africa and Europe and America to exchange or trade with less ability of government to control it, mean that in the end this advance in technology will have the greatest effect on the framework of law that governs the inter-relationships between nations. It's the greatest change since the Industrial Revolution of the late 1700s – textiles and all that – and it is difficult to see that it will have less than fundamental effects on the power of government to rule its territories.

SE: How do you see that, Ralph?

RH: I am normally optimistic and hope for the best and can see hope for the future. I am less optimistic than Arthur about the whole European entanglement. The removal of barriers to trade, the removal of barriers for the free movement of men and of capital is an excellent thing: it is the free-trade ideal of Adam Smith, which even he thought was utopian. But with the European project has come the imposition of standards, standards in the definition of products, and standards in the definition of safety and security of products, that are pitched rather high and raise costs and prices, and standards about employment. I see that as being exactly opposed to free trade, so that that worries me, and I do predict that if that were successful, then it would reduce Europe to a backwater from the rest of the world. I think I look to America, I look to China and Asia, to maintain this entrepreneurial vigour, catching up, impatience to improve. No, I think on the whole, we will survive all that.

SE: What I think I am hearing is that the twenty-first century may be more friendly to liberty than the twentieth century has been because of the spread of markets.

RH: I believe that, I do actually believe that . . .

AS: We are both saying yes for reasons which differ. I think that the power of people in markets, because of these unprecedented technological changes that the world has never seen before, will make it difficult even for the governments of larger federal unions like Australia to assert their sovereignty over their peoples and their states.

RH: Amen to that, but it depends upon . . . I am enormously impressed by the argument that the underground economy, the rebellion against government, will increasingly make it difficult for governments to impose these high taxes. The black economy is breaking all records, and a lot of the people who are registered as unemployed are actually hard at work, not only as window cleaners and car cleaners and all of that, but in quite reasonable ways of business, not least the Asian population. But the EU reaches out, this minute as we talk, in an effort to impose on the whole of Europe a withholding tax, on anyone who is receiving income from investment. Brussels says the payer should retain 20 or 30 or 40 per cent, retain it and pay a reduced outlay, in order to avoid tax evasion – it is presented as a tax-evasion measure. And so this government is faced with a battle. Is it going to allow Europe to impose this withholding tax, which, it is said, would undermine a large part of the city of London's international appeal?

AS: Thomas Hobbes has since the seventeenth century scared us all by fear that the outcome of what he said would be chaos. He taught that without sovereignty, that is government and power, there could be no civilised society but anarchy. That was a simplistic vision. It may have seemed to be true then, but what he did not say was that the power of the government, the rules of the sovereign, would have to be such as to reflect the aspirations of the people. In the seventeenth century those aspirations weren't strong enough, they weren't strong enough in the eighteenth century, nor in the nineteenth century, or in the one now ended. But in the twenty-first century I think that the power of the people will be such that if the government does not allow them to exercise the powers that markets give them, they will rebel. And they are rebelling now.

RH: I take my stand on the bedrock of human nature. I believe that man is imperfect, man is always doomed to setbacks and frustrations and struggles and re-struggles. I believe the market has something of the eternal validity of the laws of motion and the laws of gravity. I think the market, this concept of a way of bringing people together – not physically together, but linking them through phones, through brokers, through advertisements, through the internet and so forth – I believe that remains the only way for free people to accommodate themselves to one another, and to distant people of which they know little. I would not have any great utopian thoughts that the twenty-first century will solve all these problems. They will struggle on and there will be setbacks. But, this is the great hope, when living standards have risen a bit more, as they have been rising recently – we doubled our standard of living by 1980 and we were on our way to doubling it again, quadrupling compared to our youth – then I believe in the possibility that the whole of this state welfare drug will be kicked. People will see that they can afford better things for themselves, without the intermediation of government. If the state is reduced to concentrate on those things it has to do, to maintain order, to enforce contracts, to help look after those who cannot live in a free-market state because of a permanent disability, then that would be marvellous, that would be a proper balance in society.

SE: Again, it's been a real privilege to spend some time with you, and I should probably just ask you one final time if there is any particular thing that you would like to have linger with us?

AS: I think if you feel you are right you go on arguing until you are established as having told the truth. You can't live with the untruth if you feel you have found the truth.

SE: So the truth really matters, popular or not?

AS: I don't think I would have enjoyed my life apart from other aspects, if I felt that there was something I could have done, there was truth I felt I could have popularised and have an influence on the world for our friends, our country. I think it would have spoiled the enjoyment I got out of the rest of my life. I could have turned aside from this place and earned much more, at some stage much more at the brewery which would give me all the wine I wanted and the beer and where salaries were very good. It wasn't my first choice, but I could have gone on there. Ralph can speak for himself. Ralph would either have entered parliament or have ended up as the editor of *The Times*.

RH: My last quote is this. The last phase of my life is occasional attendance at the House of Lords. I meet some people there of all parties who are very considerable public figures. I discover that they will go into the lobby when voting time comes to support that for which they have no enthusiasm, to oppose that which they sometimes actually favour; and you see the extent to which important persons no longer feel themselves free to say exactly what they think. It is less bad in the House of Lords of course than the House of Commons, where they are slaves of the Whip. But it does raise up in my mind this enormous gratitude to have had what Antony Fisher called an 'independent station'. He had phrases – Antony Fisher was a Christian Scientist – and he was moved by a number of very simple adages, one of which he quoted from Archimedes: 'Give me a lever and I will move the world.' And he thought the IEA was the lever, and the fulcrum was market forces. He had another phrase: in bad times, if things were difficult, he would say – one of his sayings from his Christian Science – 'There is not enough darkness in the whole world to extinguish the light of a single candle.' And you suddenly glowed, incandescent as a candle in the pitch black. He was an enormous inspiration. You knew exactly, transparently, exactly what this man believed, and I hope he felt the same of us.

SE: Well, many of us believe that the IEA has been that candle and – how shall I put it? – the two of you have been its flame. Thank you very much for our time together.

The 42 questions were not pre-announced.

COMMENTARIES

1 Spies in the night?
Sir Alastair Burnet

They came, it seemed at the time, like spies in the night. Well, not exactly. They were polite, even courteous, plainly intelligent fellows who enjoyed an argument. Only after a bit did it become apparent that they usually won their arguments. The well-drilled ranks of us Keynesians began to suffer uncomfortable casualties. The Butskellite regiments, entrenched in the ministries and universities, had severe butchers' bills.

The intellectual concussion caused by the Institute of Economic Affairs, conducted by Ralph Harris and Arthur Seldon from 1957 onwards, upon the body politic and economic was cumulative and, eventually, decisive. Policies that were deemed to be politically impossible and unpopular by politicians, civil servants, captains of industry and the trade unions were discovered to be practical, popular and successful. Even television and the newspapers began to get the idea.

Success has many fathers, but none have better deserved the recognition and acclaim than the founding fathers of the IEA who did the work. They did the fighting. They took the risks. They had the solutions. Not all were practicable. Not all the enemies were converted or routed. But the very way of thought of the country was decisively altered. The heir to what was called Thatcherism turned out to be (despite his faults) Tony Blair. This sort of succession was not thought to be even remotely possible when the IEA began.

It gradually grasped the secret that eluded everyone else. By hard work, experience, judgement and a bit of luck along the path, it developed studies on how to get inside the very brains of the establishment, of the forces that run the country. Naturally, it took time: time to educate a new generation of young people who would rebel against the failed wisdom of the British past.

Education has been first and foremost in their policy. It was fortunate for the country that they had twenty years of effort, experience and persuasion behind them when the country found in that most depressing of decades, the 1970s, that it faced both economic bankruptcy and the intellectual bankruptcy of the political parties. The IEA had the acumen and the ability to change the very terms of the argument.

There were coming into public life then the young people who believed change was a necessity. In politics, business, university life, even in trade unions, there were young people who had caught something of the IEA's influence and teaching. Their minds were open to the freedom of thought, of trade, of purpose that the crisis needed if the country was to be shifted, bodily, on to the right track.

Instrumental in this work over the years was the IEA's splendid variety of books and publications for a wide spectrum of readerships: Hobart Papers, Hobart Paperbacks, Eaton Papers, Occasional Papers, Readings, Research Monographs and the journal *Economic Affairs*. This sustained effort called for ideas, contacts, contributors, an understanding of the market and, above all, editorship. In Arthur, the IEA had an exemplary contributor and an editor of genius. Their relations with the media have progressed from the early days when they were treated with suspicion, as an offshoot of what was supposedly the New Right. *The Times*, *Daily Telegraph* and *Financial Times* have all had senior editorial people and opinion-formers who have understood and supported the IEA's principles and ambitions. In the continuous struggle in broadcasting for airtime to voice opinions, a younger generation has come to acknowledge the value of the IEA's contributions to the national debate.

It is important to identify not only where they succeeded but where they avoided mistakes. They differed from many great causes: they were never single-issue campaigners. Unlike the Fabians, they were never committed to a single political party. The Liberals, who, historically, might have taken them up, preferred to cling to the welfare state. Labour provided some useful exponents of the IEA philosophy; they knew their working class. Thatcher and the young MPs she brought into the Commons were often persuaded about policy. She and Sir Keith Joseph were converts and paid tribute to the converters, but the Conservative Party still retained a Heathite wing. The IEA carefully separated itself from public money. It was essential to its independence.

Further, the IEA has strongly promoted its overseas connections in the economic and philosophical argument. From Friedrich von Hayek to Milton Friedman it has drawn inspiration and comfort from the influential international leaders who share its convictions. As worldwide issues have come to dominate events and controversies the IEA has exercised its guidance and leverage on policies. It is a fine record.

2 The IEA's influence in our times
Milton Friedman

Antony Fisher's decision to found the IEA in 1955, reconstructed and enlarged in 1957 by the partnership of Ralph (later Lord) Harris and Arthur Seldon, played a major role in transforming the intellectual climate of opinion in Great Britain and indeed in the world.

Ralph originally impressed Fisher at a political meeting near his home in Sussex. Arthur was recommended by Arnold Plant of the London School of Economics.

The IEA's success owes much to the way that they complemented one another – they fitted together like pieces in a jigsaw puzzle. Ralph, outgoing, hail-fellow-well-met, an excellent public speaker, was an ideal choice for the 'outside'. Arthur was an exacting academic with a passion for precision, the ideal choice for the 'inside' role. Ralph was a brilliant voice of the institute; Arthur an unrelenting enforcer of intellectual standards in the Institute's books and the celebrated Hobart Papers he created. Ralph's interest in the politics of economics balanced Arthur's in the economics of politics.

Had the IEA never existed, Margaret Thatcher might still have become Prime Minister, but the reforms she presided over would not have been politically feasible, and most likely would not even have been part of her platform. Seldom does a country, to plagiarise Winston Churchill, owe so much to so few.

The IEA was successful because it did not seek short-term influence. Ralph and Arthur maintained a firm policy of sticking to well-defined principles, presenting ideas conforming to those principles regardless of their apparent political feasibility or their acceptability to current vested interests. High intellectual quality, firm and clearly stated principles, absence of narrow political partisanship, stress on the long run, and vigorous but unbiased scholarly exposition – these were the hallmarks of the Institute. And these are the qualities that enabled it to play such a vital role in the intellectual life of Britain and the wider world.

The IEA's influence has not been confined to the United Kingdom. Its publications and the able group of scholars who became associated with it contributed greatly to the change in the intellectual climate of opinion around the world. More concretely, a large number of similar institutes have been established in many countries, under the stimulus of their example and sometimes with Fisher's direct assistance and encouragement. These institutes have disseminated publications and ideas developed at the IEA.

More important, they have produced economic studies applying general free-market principles to the specific problems of their own countries. In the process, just as Harris and Seldon did in Britain, they have nurtured in each country a group of academics and non-academics effectively promoting and exploring the principles of human and economic freedom. And, just as in Britain, they transformed the intellectual climate so that today free-market policies are feasible that were once regarded as unthinkable.

I owe a great personal debt to Harris and Seldon. For decades they have provided me at the IEA with an intellectual home away from home. Through them I have been able to meet and communicate with individuals in the political community, the journalistic community and the academic community, to some of whom I might not otherwise have had access. Under their sponsorship I have been able to talk and publish and to reach the intellectual community in Europe. And reciprocally, the seminars at the IEA and the personal and private discussions with Ralph in London and also with Arthur at our homes in Vermont and Kent altered my own views, and enabled me to clarify some issues better than I otherwise would.

As veterans of a major 30-year intellectual battle dating back to the end of World War II, and in the phalanx of people who have promoted ideas of freedom and human liberty, Ralph Harris and Arthur Seldon deserve a place of honour.

3 The IEA and its indirect influence abroad
Herbert Giersch

British socialist thought had been intellectual food for me in various places: as a prisoner of war in England during the famine of 1945/46, as an undernourished citizen of the British Occupation Zone in Germany in 1947 and as a British Council Fellow at the LSE in London in 1948. Such experience made me first choice as an interpreter for a group of German economists visiting England in 1949.

They were to be made acquainted with Oxford and Cambridge thinking on full employment and with the socialists' apparent victory in the debate on 'economic calculation'. I might have been persuaded by the stuff I had to translate if I had not become immunised shortly before in long discussions at the LSE with Hayek and Robbins, Popper and Paish, Peacock and Plant.

I did not yet know Arthur Seldon and Ralph Harris at the IEA. As a substitute for being exposed to their ideas I had come under the spell of a miraculous experience in Germany: the sudden change of economic life when Ludwig Erhard, the still obscure economics professor responsible for economic policy in the Anglo-American Bi-Zone, supplemented the 1948 currency reform by defying the Allied Control Commission and lifting many of the controls that had fettered the body economic. No academic research institution could then have had such an impact on people's minds. The Erhard experiment turned out to become the 'German lesson' for about a generation.

At the same time that the miracle on the Continent lost its glamour and began to fade, Arthur Seldon and Ralph Harris entered the scene in Britain and gained ground in demonstrating that ideas can be as powerful as events, provided they fairly soon find persuasive protagonists and followers. What Erhard's experiment had shown to the population of Germany, Margaret Thatcher and Keith Joseph learned to preach and practised as a medicine for Britain, but they could do so only after the ground had been prepared by the IEA and its founders. Looking back over more than half a century, I find it fascinating to observe how deeply ideas can change the world of politics and economics.

That is the lesson of the IEA. It proved to be an exciting example to show how two forces of history can act in tandem, one in the world of practical evidence, the other in the world of economic ideas. The outcome is striking. Germany, over the last fifty years, has become an economic powerhouse once again. Yet, on closer inspection, it showed dangerous symptoms of institutional sclerosis after only two decades of reconstruction. In Britain, Margaret Thatcher presided over a process of regeneration, reforming itself in the wake of a genuine intellectual revolution. Congratulations!

I must confess to having originally held the naive view that no country or organisation can rejuvenate itself without a salutary shock from outside. Here, I gladly admit to having been wrong: rejuvenation is possible if people can be taught to adopt a paradigm shift. But it needs to be sustained by enthusiasm. Ideas of freedom are contagious. Though Arthur and Ralph did not specifically act as missionaries in other countries, their successful example encouraged similar endeavours of scholarly persuasion and enlightenment abroad, particularly in those countries on the European continent which were eager to find their way from socialism to free society.

For present-day Germany, my advice must be: look at Britain today as a 'model' country. Offering more freedom than under Old Labour, Britain has once again succeeded in overtaking Germany on the march to prosperity. And it is likely to move faster in the years ahead. Again, congratulations, Britannia!

Germany would be well advised to learn from this change. But who is competent and willing to play the roles of Lord Harris and Arthur Seldon on the Continent, particularly in East Germany, where people have been subject to communist indoctrination for 45 years?

The IEA under Arthur and Ralph was highly successful. But to achieve its objectives it required generous support, both financial and intellectual. In making their impact on public opinion in Britain they could rely on strong impulses from the world of ideas, notably from two of the greatest worldly philosophers of the last century: the Austrian-British Friedrich Hayek and the American Milton Friedman. They also built an increasing intellectual army of younger British economists who applied classical liberalism to a widening range of British economic life. That process has spread to most English-speaking countries but not yet to the countries of continental Europe.

4 A team of singular impact

Peter Hennessy

This is a wonderfully evocative video which brings out the full flavour of two free and pioneering spirits who formed a team of singular impact.

Events shift conventional wisdoms, but new/old notions can form or reform effectively only if ideas people have established the rudiments of a new intellectual climate well in advance. Ralph Harris and Arthur Seldon turned out to be two of the most significant weather-makers in the post-war history of British political economy over the 30 years from the start of their partnership in 1957.

As pioneers in the period when it was tough to be on the receiving end of the prevailing mixed economy/welfare state consensus, they have the respect of people like me who do not share all of what Harris calls their 'full frontal' opinions and analyses. They are very different in temperament and values from the jumpers-on-to-bandwagons of the 1980s who hurtled so determinedly to the aid of the electoral victrix in the Thatcher years.

Economic history should accord an inseparability to Harris and Seldon comparable to that which musicologists have conferred on Gilbert and Sullivan.

5 *Yes, Minister* and the IEA

Sir Antony Jay

I spent the first nine years of my working life on the staff of the BBC, as a trainee, a producer, an editor, and finally head of department in the Current Affairs Group. I was a perfect anthology of neo-liberal attitudes. Like virtually all my colleagues I was anti-advertising, anti-capitalism, anti-industry, anti-monarchy, anti-selling, anti-authority, anti-profit; whatever made the world a freer and more prosperous place, you name it, I was anti-it. And then something happened. Or rather a number of things happened.

First, I left the BBC in the spring of 1964 to freelance as a writer and producer. Second, the Wilson government was elected. Third, I started to make films for business corporations. And fourth, my first book was published.

These events led to a lot of discoveries. As a freelance I discovered that the first necessity was to bring in the money. (In the BBC, the audience supplied the money and could be fined or jailed if they refused, a sanction regrettably not available to the freelance writer.) Selling became a survival skill. The Wilson government demonstrated that the 'neo-liberal' principles and sentiments that furnish the rhetoric of opposition are a deep embarrassment when confronting the realities of government – a lesson being learnt all over again by Robin Cook with his 'ethical' foreign policy. Working with business corporations taught me that businessmen, for the most part, were not greedy, unprincipled exploiters of the unsuspecting consumer, but decent people struggling to make a living and stay out of the hands of the official receiver. And having my book published made me a sort of entrepreneur, writing jacket copy as eagerly as any agency copywriter.

All these revelations were brought into focus when I was invited to speak to the Headmasters' Conference in 1971. My central argument was addressed to those 'neo-liberal' ideas I had taken with me from St Paul's and Cambridge to the BBC and which were shared by so many of my Oxbridge colleagues in the corporation. I pointed out that the school fees that kept headmasters in business came from industry, and that their distaste for and disparagement of the world of business and industry was a kamikaze philosophy. I doubt if it had much effect on the distinguished gathering for which it was intended, but it had a result which transformed my political philosophy more profoundly and permanently than anything before or since. My speech was broadcast on Radio 4, and the morning after transmission a stranger calling himself Ralph Harris rang and invited me to lunch at the Institute of Economic Affairs.

I found myself almost in a *Samizdat* world, a secret and subversive cell where heresies were propounded and revolutionary pamphlets were circulated. One that came into my hands quite early on was an extensive *Playboy* interview with Milton Friedman. I read it with tremendous intellectual excitement. All my adult life I had been irritated by economics and quite unable to understand it. Phrases like 'deficit budgeting' and 'aggregate demand' did not seem to relate to anything I understood. And then suddenly, reading the Friedman article, I discovered that I could understand economics after all.

It all fitted together. It made sense. Exposure to the IEA reading list showed me the futility of government planning, the role of competition, the operation of the price mechanism, the harnessing of self-interest to the public good, the function of markets and their spontaneity (later demonstrated by car-boot sales), the fallacy of government attempts to control prices and incomes, and the reason why the economic democracy of the supermarket is so much more sensitive and effective than the quinquennial referenda we call 'general elections': why Westminster's ballot boxes are so much less efficient that Tesco's checkouts, especially in serving the wishes of minorities.

Unlike the economics I had been failing to understand all my life, the economics I learnt at the IEA not only made complete sense of the economic world as I had observed and experienced it; it also fitted together as a complete system that was consistent, logical, and above all moral. It showed that capitalism was a better guarantee of freedom, justice and equality than the welfare state with its bureaucratised charity and subcontracted compassion. This understanding was reinforced when Milton Friedman was looking for a company to produce his television series *Free to Choose*. Having failed to find any company in America whose producers could understand what he was talking about, he called Ralph in desperation to ask if he knew anyone in the UK who could do the job. Ralph put him on to my company, and the resulting co-operation (apart from producing an extremely popular television series) gave me the opportunity of many long conversations with Milton and Rose which amounted to extended tutorials in market economics from one of the world's leading exponents.

In parallel with this growing understanding of the virtues of the free market came understanding of the follies, fallacies and failures of government's attempts to interfere with it. The key insight was that, for governments, the public good was not an objective but a constraint. The objective of politicians was re-election; the objective of civil servants was a comfortable life, a good salary, authority, status and the eventual KCB. Insofar as these could not be achieved without some regard to the public interest, some consideration had to be given to it, but it was not the primary objective nor the principal reward. And since the rewards for cabinet ministers were not only different from but often in conflict with those of permanent secretaries, the result was frequent collision and collusion in the corridors of power. In those days, around 1977, I had not yet encountered the discipline of Public Choice Economics, but I understood its implications and could see its comedy potential. This insight was the underlying theme of *Yes, Minister* and *Yes, Prime Minister*, and I have no hesitation in acknowledging my debt to Ralph Harris and Arthur Seldon and their IEA colleagues for their role in its conception.

There is a sense in which *Yes, Minister* was out of date before it appeared. The first transmission was in 1980, at the start of the Thatcher years, and the last in 1987. Those were the years of conviction politics, of market principles, and of the attempt to rescue government from the Slough of Dirigisme. But Jim Hacker, the Minister/PM, belonged to the previous epoch, the Heath/Wilson years, the years of opinion-poll driven, media-focused, interventionist government. Those years are back again, and the TV programmes are in a sense more topical now than when they were first transmitted.

But in another sense they went out at the right time. If they had a message (and it was certainly never our intention to include one) it was that those in political power are neither organised nor motivated to serve the public interest. The corollary is that people are best left alone as far as possible, to pursue their own objectives, in their own way, with their own money. That is something I have learnt through my connection with the IEA, and even if that were all it would still be a cause for profound gratitude.

6 Stupor mundi: the IEA and its impact
Antonio Martino

The Revolution

The twentieth century was the century of the state, a century of dictators, the century of Hitler and Stalin, as well as the century of arbitrary government and of unprecedented intrusion of politics into daily lives. It has produced the largest increase in the size of government in the history of mankind.

In 1900 the ratio of government spending to gross domestic product in Italy was 10 per cent, in the 1950s 30 per cent, and it is now roughly 50 per cent. Similar statistics apply to most countries in Europe. In this sense, a prophecy has been confirmed. The entry 'Fascism' in the *Enciclopaedia Italiana*, signed by Benito Mussolini, reads: 'The nineteenth century has been the century of the individual (for liberalism means individualism); it may be conjectured that this is the century of the state ... the century of authority, a Fascist century.'

For the greatest part of the century the prevailing intellectual climate has been in favour of socialism in one form or another. The future of freedom, of a society based on voluntary cooperation, free markets and the rule of law appeared uncertain. At the Mont Pèlerin Society meeting in Hillsdale in 1975 a prominent member of the society was convinced that England would become a dictatorship in five years. Though many on the British left would probably say his prediction was confirmed by the advent of Mrs Thatcher, this kind of pessimism proved to be excessive: today, while socialism appears destined to fade away, capitalism is very much alive and there is a widespread revival of understanding and praise for the free enterprise system, even among historic opponents.

The epochal change in public policy began as an intellectual revolution. On the practical importance of their ideas, economists disagree. While Keynes was very sanguine, George Stigler of Chicago was convinced that the practical relevance of the economists' intellectual output was minimal. In my mind 'the Great U-turn' of our times has been initiated by a legendary revolution in economic thinking. From the perspective of the ideological confrontation – thanks to the dissemination of the ideas of the great liberal scholars of the twentieth century – we live in one of the happiest times in the history of mankind. Never before has the case for freedom been more thoroughly analysed and better understood. And more people are aware of the importance of freedom today than at any other time in the past fifty or hundred years.

This is a strong statement. Few people who are great thinkers in the eyes of their contemporaries stand the test of time and are still considered great by future generations. As a result, we are often led to believe that there are more great scholars among our contemporaries than there were in the past. Yet a very large number of the great liberal thinkers of all times belong to the twentieth century. Furthermore, even though ideas can be traced back to past achievements, the case for freedom as presented by today's thinkers is more consistently argued and better supported than ever before.

The IEA

The Institute of Economic Affairs is probably the most conclusive example of the power of ideas. Drawing on the output of contemporary liberal giants from many countries like the British-Austrian Hayek, the American Friedman, the Scottish-American Buchanan and Tullock, and promoting original research on contemporary issues by young British academics new to classical liberalism, the IEA provided intellectual ammunition for freedom fighters all over the world.

The IEA's publications were invariably relevant, rigorous and readable. In the dark years of the socialist consensus, they gave courage to the unconvinced and sowed doubts in the minds of believers. Gradually, at first imperceptibly, then with increasing effectiveness, their output started first to be noticed, then to be discussed, and finally, over twenty to thirty years, to make a difference. We have an immense debt of gratitude for what it has done, for its persistence, especially in the first decades of its existence, and for the very high scholarly quality of its products. I still keep all the IEA's publications in my room, and look at some of the older ones with affection. They remind me of the time when most economists were convinced that inflation was the unavoidable price of economic growth and a cure for unemployment – when it was thought possible to reduce interest rates through monetary expansion and to 'fine-tune' the economy in the short term, thus avoiding the ups and downs of the economic cycle.

At that time, inflation was not considered a monetary phenomenon but the result of excessive increases in wages, so that in order to combat inflation governments had to resort to wage and price controls, come to terms with the unions and pursue expansionary monetary and fiscal policies to stimulate demand. All of this sounds absurd today, and it certainly is, but it was the general consensus at the time, shared by the Labour Party and to a large extent by the Tories. Everybody seemed to agree with the same Keynesian concoction: easy money, high taxation, deficit spending, and wage and price controls (or incomes policy, as it was called in England). The IEA was the exception. Its output of books and papers on an awe-inspiring range of subjects was decades ahead of the time. It was refreshing to read its publications as soon as they arrived.

'A university professor is someone who thinks otherwise,' runs a German adage. Thanks to the IEA we have kept on thinking otherwise in the face of the cold gale of conformism. Today we can finally enjoy the widespread acceptance of what in the past were thought to be our heresies.

We cannot afford to relax: we must continue refining our case, making it more convincing, exploring new ways to enlarge our freedoms.

Our fight will never end.

7 The IEA and the advance to classical liberalism

Pascal Salin

The video conversation between Ralph Harris, Arthur Seldon and Stephen Erickson is a fascinating document. It shows how a couple of clear-sighted and resolute young men could have a great influence on the intellectual environment and the policies of their country; it explains how ideas – those of Friedrich Hayek and others – have consequences. These men show the way to others, for instance when Arthur Seldon says: 'The great debt that academics owe society is to speak the truth, even if it's untimely, and awkward, and even if it risks their jobs.' Given the great achievement of Harris, Seldon and the Institute of Economic Affairs, I am particularly happy to have the opportunity to contribute some personal thoughts.

As a university professor, I receive a lot of costly publications published by governments, central banks and international organisations (at the taxpayer's expense). I cannot remember having ever extracted any new idea from looking at these publications. The contrast with the publications of the IEA is amazing. All its booklets and books offer new ideas, new perspectives, pathbreaking thoughts, precious information! What is extraordinary is that this outstanding intellectual enterprise was produced for so many years by only two 'entrepreneurs', helped by limited but dedicated staff. Just imagine what would have happened with a government-managed think tank. The staff would have expanded to hundreds of people (mainly in the administrative sector), working in a huge building, spending an ever-increasing budget, using more and more powerful computers, and producing lots of statistics and econometric computations without caring about the desirability of this production. The IEA proved – under the management of

Ralph Harris and Arthur Seldon – that one can be faithful to one's own principles, that it is possible to wield extensive influence without extensive expenditure, that a small group of people can really change the course of economic life for millions of others.

Even if I am impressed by all I know about the impact of the IEA, I am certainly not the best suited to evaluate the precise influence it has had in the UK, and I leave this task to my British colleagues. But I would like to stress that this influence has not been limited to the borders of the UK. For all those who felt intellectually isolated in their own country, the IEA booklets and books have been a fantastic source of inspiration, of information, of motivation. Moreover, the IEA has been the model under which so many institutes and think tanks have been created all over the world. It may be impossible to surpass the IEA, and it may remain a model for a long time. It had a unique role in the rebirth of liberal ideas in the world during the second half of the twentieth century. And, looking back to the intellectual climate which prevailed in the whole world some decades ago, one cannot but admire the courage and the lucidity of the IEA people (as well as those of the most famous like Friedrich Hayek or Milton Friedman). We must be grateful to them for having so deeply transformed the intellectual scenery, even if so much remains to be done (especially in a country like mine, France, where the lack of an IEA is strongly felt).

At this point may I add a personal recollection? When François Mitterand was elected as President of the Republic in May 1981, I was deeply disturbed and the first thing I did was to call Harris. He comforted me by giving me the vision of the long run. And it is true that one has to be optimistic when comparing the intellectual and political atmosphere in the UK in the 1950s – which Ralph Harris and Arthur Seldon revive so clearly in their video conversation – and the present achievements. In France we are politically still in about the same situation as the one which prevailed in the UK in the fifties.

There may be changes in French public opinion as its younger generations become more open to classical liberalism. But much has to be done. When I had the chance to meet Lady Thatcher some years ago, under the friendly auspices of the IEA, she told me, 'Oh! You are French! You need someone like me in France!' She was certainly right. But, before getting a Thatcher, we first need a Harris and a Seldon. That is the best I could wish for my country.

8 The intellectual situation in the United States in the post-war years and the influence of the IEA
Gordon Tullock

When I came out of the army in 1946 and went back to law school at the University of Chicago, I found an intellectual climate very similar to that faced by Harris and Seldon in Britain. It was however less extreme. Since I had originally been an old-fashioned conservative and had been converted to a Chicago-type conservative by Henry Simons, I was unhappy. I do not wish to exaggerate. Most of my classmates were simply planning to make money in the law. They had not, however, adopted the Chicago conservative position and were either mild socialists or uninterested in such matters.

Under the circumstances I thought that the world was going socialist. I disliked this but I did not feel that there was much I could do about it. In consequence I decided that I would have to make a career in government rather than in the market. Black reactionary that I was, I thought that the government should handle foreign affairs and hence my personal feelings would not be injured by a career in the Department of State. I therefore became a diplomat. I should say that my initial experience in China where I was 'liberated' by the Chinese People's Liberation Army and then went on to serve in various posts and positions dealing with the Chinese communists reinforced my feeling that the market was better than socialism.

That I felt more or less alone in this feeling until about 1960 meant that I had no sense that the trend would be reversed. I did make contact with von Mises and Popper and I heard a few lectures by Hayek and Friedman, so I realised that there were major intellects on my side. Further, the *National Review* had begun publication. Still, I felt very much alone.

At about this time a free-enterprise research outfit, the Princeton Panel, was established and they hired me. As a result I heard about the Institute of Economic Affairs, which had, although I did not realise it immediately, inspired the Princeton efforts. I met Peter Bauer who visited Princeton. Antony Fisher also passed through and I exchanged a few words with him. Unfortunately financial matters led to the winding-up of the Princeton Panel almost before it got started. I ended up teaching international studies at the University of South Carolina. The man who hired me was a China expert and an anti-communist, but with little or no knowledge of or interest in economics.

At this time, I visited London and was much impressed to see Institute of Economic Affairs pamphlets on display at the *Economist*'s bookstore, right beside the Labour Party's pamphlets. I also met Seldon and Harris and had lunch in their famous lunch room. Thus I no longer felt so much alone. I also began reading their output and was much impressed.

One example of their influence was Arthur Seldon's spending the summer in Washington assisting the American Enterprise Institute's publication programme. I do not know exactly what he did, but the results were very significant. Readability and topicality of the AEI's output greatly increased. Since at the time they were almost the only opponent of the Brookings Institution, this was a significant advance.

So far my remarks have been mainly autobiographical. I suspect however that I was not alone and that there were many other people who were similarly affected. I am, in a way, a sample drawn from a much larger universe. Thus the Institute's impact on somebody who was a minor academic figure in a minor university is merely a sample of its total impact.

That impact has grown. There are now versions of the Institute of Economic Affairs all over the world. For some reason the project does not seem to have been very successful in Latin countries, but elsewhere it has been immensely important. To give but one example, there are now several institutes in Washington following in the footsteps of Seldon and Harris, and we are developing a large number of state copies. It is not true that we have fifty yet, but I suspect we will have.

It is not just propaganda. Britain had a Prime Minister (the best man among them) who was directly under the influence of the Institute, Seldon and Harris. President Reagan had a number of free-market types in his cabinet. The head of his OMB was one of my students. Further, although President Reagan was not a great scholar, he did understand policy making and did a good job with it. Both Thatcher and Reagan realised that politically there were restrictions on what they could do, but they did a lot.

To repeat what I said at the beginning, in the late 1940s and 1950s the situation was deeply discouraging. That has changed. For the change we can thank, to a large extent, Antony Fisher, Arthur Seldon and Ralph Harris. The world owes them an immense debt of gratitude. They showed that we should not become discouraged when things look hopeless. Hard work, intelligence, and persuasive ability do work. The world is a better place as a result.

ABOUT THE IEA

The Institute is a research and educational charity (No. CC 235 351), limited by guarantee. Its mission is to improve understanding of the fundamental institutions of a free society with particular reference to the role of markets in solving economic and social problems.

The IEA achieves its mission by:

- a high quality publishing programme
- conferences, seminars, lectures and other events
- outreach to school and college students
- brokering media introductions and appearances

The IEA, which was established in 1955 by the late Sir Antony Fisher, is an educational charity, not a political organisation. It is independent of any political party or group and does not carry on activities intended to affect support for any political party or candidate in any election or referendum, or at any other time. It is financed by sales of publications, conference fees and voluntary donations.

In addition to its main series of publications the IEA also publishes a quarterly journal, *Economic Affairs*, and has two specialist programmes – Environment and Technology, and Education.

The IEA is aided in its work by a distinguished international Academic Advisory Council and an eminent panel of Honorary Fellows. Together with other academics, they review prospective IEA publications, their comments being passed on anonymously to authors. All IEA papers are therefore subject to the same rigorous independent refereeing process as used by leading academic journals.

IEA publications enjoy widespread classroom use and course adoptions in schools and universities. They are also sold throughout the world and often translated/reprinted.

Since 1974 the IEA has helped to create a world-wide network of 100 similar institutions in over 70 countries. They are all independent but share the IEA's mission.

Views expressed in the IEA's publications are those of the authors, not those of the Institute (which has no corporate view), its Managing Trustees, Academic Advisory Council members or senior staff.

Members of the Institute's Academic Advisory Council, Honorary Fellows, Trustees and Staff are listed on the following page.

The Institute gratefully acknowledges financial support for its publications programme and other work from a generous benefaction by the late Alec and Beryl Warren.

The Institute of Economic Affairs
2 Lord North Street, Westminster, London SW1P 3LB
Tel: 020 7799 8900
Fax: 020 7799 2137
Email: iea@iea.org.uk
Internet: iea.org.uk

General Director	John Blundell
Editorial Director	Professor Colin Robinson

Managing Trustees

Chairman: Sir Peter Walters
Robert Boyd
Michael Fisher
Malcolm McAlpine
Professor D R Myddelton
Sir Michael Richardson

Professor Martin Ricketts
Lord Vinson, LVO
Linda Whetstone
Professor Geoffrey E Wood

Academic Advisory Council

Chairman: Professor Martin Ricketts
Graham Bannock
Professor Norman Barry
Professor Michael Beenstock
Professor John Burton
Professor Forrest Capie
Professor Steven N S Cheung
Professor Tim Congdon
Professor N F R Crafts
Professor David de Meza
Professor Richard A Epstein
Nigel Essex
John Flemming
Professor David Greenaway
Walter E Grinder
Professor Steve H Hanke
Professor Keith Hartley
Dr R M Hartwell
Professor Peter M Jackson
Dr Jerry Jordan
Professor Daniel B Klein
Dr Anja Kluever

Professor David Laidler
Professor Stephen C Littlechild
Professor Antonio Martino
Dr Ingrid A Merikoski
Professor Patrick Minford
Professor David Parker
Professor Victoria Curzon Price
Professor Charles K Rowley
Professor Pascal Salin
Professor Pedro Schwartz
Professor J R Shackleton
Jane S Shaw
Professor W Stanley Siebert
Professor David Simpson
Professor Vernon L Smith
Professor Nicola Tynan
Professor Roland Vaubel
Professor E G West
Professor Lawrence H White
Professor Walter E Williams

Honorary Fellows

Professor Armen A Alchian
Sir Samuel Brittan
Professor James M Buchanan
Professor Ronald H Coase
Professor Terence W Hutchison
Professor Dennis S Lees
Professor Chiaki Nishiyama

Professor Sir Alan Peacock
Professor Ivor Pearce
Professor Ben Roberts
Professor Anna J Schwartz
Professor Gordon Tullock
Professor Sir Alan Walters
Professor Basil S Yamey

Other papers recently published by the IEA include:

WHO, What and Why?
Transnational Government, Legitimacy and the World Health Organization
Roger Scruton
Occasional Paper 113
ISBN 0 255 36487 3

The World Turned Rightside Up
A New Trading Agenda for the Age of Globalisation
John C. Hulsman
Occasional Paper 114
ISBN 0 255 36495 4

The Representation of Business in English Literature
Introduced and edited by Arthur Pollard
Readings 53
ISBN 0 255 36491 1

Anti-Liberalism 2000
The Rise of New Millennium Collectivism
David Henderson
Occasional Paper 115
ISBN 0 255 36497 0

Capitalism, Morality and Markets
Brian Griffiths, Robert A. Sirico, Norman Barry and Frank Field
Readings 54
ISBN 0 255 36496 2

Malaria and the DDT Story
Richard Tren and Roger Bate
Occasional Paper 117
ISBN 0 255 36499 7

To order copies of currently available IEA papers, or to enquire about availability, please contact:

Lavis Marketing
73 Lime Walk
Oxford OX3 7AD

Tel: 01865 767575
Fax: 01865 750079
Email: orders@lavismarketing.co.uk